THE DAY LENNY THE LION LOST HIS ROAR

Audley J. Young

Copyright © 2024 Audley J. Young

All rights reserved.

ISBN: 9798337572260

DEDICATION

To all the little ones who learn that true strength lies in kindness and to the grown-ups who guide them with gentle wisdom.

May your hearts always roar with compassion and your lives be filled with the joy of helping others.

ACKNOWLEDGMENTS

Creating this book has been a journey filled with love, laughter, and learning. To my family, thank you for your endless encouragement and for always reminding me of the importance of sharing, not just in the little things but in every aspect of life.

I thank the Almighty God, for the creativity and talent He gives, enabling limitless expression through creativity.

A special thank you to the educators and parents who inspire children every day, to embrace the values of kindness, friendship, and generosity. Your dedication to nurturing these virtues in the next generation is truly admirable.

To my readers, both young and gentle in heart, thank you for joining "Lenny the Lion" on his life changing adventure. I hope his tale brings as much joy to you as it has brought to me in creating it.

With gratitude,

Audley J. Young

In the heart of a beautiful, green jungle, there lived a lion named Lenny. Lenny was no ordinary lion—he was the king of the jungle! He had the loudest, strongest roar anyone had ever heard.

When Lenny roared, the trees shook, the birds flew away and all the animals bowed down to him. "ROAR!" Lenny would say, and everyone knew the king was there.

But Lenny had a problem. He loved to show off his roar a little too much. "I am the strongest! I am the bravest! I am the loudest!" he would boast to anyone who would listen.

One bright and sunny morning, Lenny woke up with a big yawn. He was ready to start his day by showing off his mighty roar. He opened his mouth wide, took a deep breath, and...

Nothing came out! Not a single sound. Lenny tried again. He took an even bigger breath, puffed out his chest, and...still nothing! Lenny had lost his roar!

"Oh no!" Lenny thought, his eyes wide with worry. "How will everyone know I'm the king without my roar?" He quickly rushed through the jungle to find his friends, hoping they could help.

The first friend Lenny met was Ellie the elephant. Ellie was wise and kind, and Lenny was sure she would have the answer. "Ellie, Ellie! I've lost my roar! What should I do?" Lenny asked, almost in tears.

Ellie gently wrapped her trunk around Lenny and said, "Lenny, you don't need a roar to be our friend. You can be kind and helpful instead." Lenny was puzzled. "But I'm the king! How will anyone listen to me?" he asked.

Ellie smiled and replied, "Maybe it's time you listened to others for a change." Lenny thought about this as he walked away. He had never thought about listening before.

Next, Lenny went to see Gina the giraffe. Gina was tall and graceful, always calm and gentle. "Gina, Gina! I've lost my roar! How can I be the king without it?" Lenny asked, his voice shaky.

Gina bent her long neck down to Lenny's level and said, "Lenny, being king isn't just about being loud. It's about caring for others too. Lenny felt sad and asked: "how will I be the bravest if I can't roar"

Gina smiled warmly and said, "True bravery is helping others, even when it's hard." Lenny nodded, still unsure but starting to understand. Maybe there was more to being king than just his roar.

As the day went on, Lenny walked through the jungle, feeling a little lost without his roar. But then, something caught his eye. Two small cubs had climbed too high in a tree and were stuck!

Without thinking, Lenny rushed over. He used his strong paws to carefully guide the two little cubs down to safety. The cubs hugged Lenny and said, "Thank you, Lenny! You're so strong and kind!"

As he rested under the shade of a tree, Lenny smiled and thought "even without my roar I can help someone." Maybe Ellie and Gina were right. Maybe there was more to being king than just being loud.

As Lenny continued his walk, he noticed the river was running low. The animals were struggling to find enough water to drink. Lenny thought for a moment and then had an idea.

He led the animals to a new spot where the water was still deep and cool. "Thank you, Lenny!" the animals cheered. They were happy, and Lenny felt proud—not because of his roar, but because he had helped.

Later that day, Lenny came across a hungry rabbit searching for food. Lenny was glad to share his own meal with the rabbit. The rabbit smiled and said, "You're a true friend, Lenny."

As the sun began to set, Lenny felt tired but happy. He had spent the whole day helping others and it felt good. Maybe being king wasn't about being loud and strong. Maybe it was about being kind, brave and helpful.

That night, as Lenny lay down under the twinkling stars, he thought about all he had learned. Just then, he felt a tickle in his throat. He opened his mouth, took a deep breath, and...ROAR! His mighty roar was back!

But this time, Lenny didn't rush to show it off. Instead, he smiled to himself, knowing that even without his roar, he could still be a great king—one who was strong in kindness, brave in helping and loud in listening.

And from that day on, Lenny roared a little less, listened a little more and the jungle was a happier place for everyone. The animals all knew that Lenny was the best king they could ever have. It was not because of his mighty roar but because of his big heart.

Moral of the story:

True strength isn't just about being the loudest or the strongest; it's about being kind, helping others, and listening with an open heart.

The End

- Bonus Activities -

Discussion Questions

1. **Why was Lenny proud of his roar?**
   - How did he feel when he lost it?
2. **What did Ellie the elephant suggest to Lenny when he lost his roar?**
   - How do you think listening to others can make you a better friend?
3. **Gina the giraffe said that being king isn't just about being loud. What did she mean?**
   - Can you think of ways you can show you care for others?
4. **How did Lenny help the two cubs who were stuck on the rock?**
   - What does this tell us about Lenny, even without his roar?
5. **Lenny found a way to help the animals find water. Why was this important?**
   - How can helping others make you feel good inside?
6. **What did Lenny learn about being a good king?**
   - Do you think being kind is more important than being strong? Why?
7. **At the end of the story, Lenny got his roar back. How did he act differently after that?**
   - Why do you think he didn't show off his roar anymore?
8. **How did the jungle change after Lenny started roaring less and listening more?**
   - How can you make your home or school a happier place?
9. **What do you think the moral of the story is?**

- How can you apply this lesson in your own life?

10. If you were Lenny, what would you have done when you lost your roar?
    - Would you ask for help or try to solve the problem on your own?

These questions encourage children to think deeply about the story's themes and relate them to their own experiences and behaviors.

Activity Suggestions

These activities are designed to reinforce the story's themes and encourage creativity, critical thinking, and empathy. These activities provide a mix of creative, physical, and reflective tasks that will help children connect with the story and its moral lessons in meaningful ways.

1. **Roar Like Lenny: Voice and Listening Game**
   - **Instructions:** Have the children take turns being "Lenny" and roaring as loud as they can. Then, explain that Lenny learned it's important to listen, too. Play a listening game where one child makes a soft sound (like clapping hands or tapping a drum), and the others must guess the sound with their eyes closed.
   - **Purpose:** This activity helps children understand the importance of balancing speaking out and listening to others.

2. **Create Your Own Jungle King/Queen Crown**
   - **Materials:** Paper, markers, crayons, scissors (with supervision), glue, and stickers.
   - **Instructions:** Have the children design and decorate their own crowns. As they work, talk about what makes someone a good king or queen. Encourage them to write or draw one kind thing they can do for others on their crown.
   - **Purpose:** This craft reinforces the idea that being a leader means being kind and caring.

3. **Role-Play: Helping Others**
   - **Instructions:** Set up different scenarios where children can act out helping others, just like Lenny did. For example, "A friend needs help tying their shoes" or "Someone dropped their book on the floor." Children take turns playing the roles of the helper and the person in need.
   - **Purpose:** This activity encourages empathy and teaches the importance of helping others.

4. **Draw Your Favorite Scene**
   - **Materials:** Paper, crayons, colored pencils, markers.
   - **Instructions:** Ask the children to draw their favorite part of the story. Once they finish, have them explain why they chose that scene and what it taught them about kindness, bravery, or listening.
   - **Purpose:** This allows children to express their creativity

and reflect on the story's themes.

5. **Jungle Animal Charades**
    - **Instructions:** Write the names of different jungle animals on pieces of paper (e.g., lion, elephant, giraffe, monkey). Children take turns picking an animal and acting it out without using words while the others guess. Afterward, discuss how each animal in the story showed kindness or bravery.
    - **Purpose:** This fun game helps reinforce the story's lessons while allowing children to use their imagination.

6. **Kindness Chain**
    - **Materials:** Strips of colored paper, markers, tape or glue.
    - **Instructions:** Each child writes or draws an act of kindness they can do for someone else on a strip of paper. Connect the strips to make a "Kindness Chain." Hang the chain in the classroom or reading area to remind everyone of the story's message.
    - **Purpose:** This collaborative activity encourages children to think of specific ways they can be kind in their daily lives.

7. **Story Retelling with Puppets**
    - **Materials:** Paper bags, socks, or craft sticks, markers, fabric scraps, glue.
    - **Instructions:** Have the children create simple puppets of Lenny, Ellie, Gina, and the cubs. Once the puppets are ready, let the children use them to retell the story, adding their own dialogue or twists.
    - **Purpose:** This activity helps with story comprehension and allows children to explore the narrative creatively.

8. **Lenny's Roar and Quiet Time Chart**
    - **Instructions:** Create a chart with two columns: "Roar Time" and "Quiet Time." Throughout the day or week, track when the children use their "Roar" voices (when it's okay to be loud) and their "Quiet" voices (when they listen or help others). Discuss how both are important.
    - **Purpose:** This activity helps children understand the importance of balancing loud, energetic moments with quiet, thoughtful ones.

9. **Jungle Kindness Parade**
    - **Instructions:** Organize a "Jungle Kindness Parade" where each child dresses up as their favorite jungle animal from the story. As they march, have them say or act out a kind thing they can do, just like Lenny did in the story.
    - **Purpose:** This fun activity allows children to physically

express the story's lessons and celebrate the value of kindness.

10. Design a New Cover
- **Materials:** Paper, markers, crayons, stickers.
- **Instructions:** Have the children design a new book cover for "The Day Lenny the Lion Lost His Roar." Encourage them to think about what image would best show the story's message.
- **Purpose:** This encourages children to think about the story's themes and how to visually represent them.

ABOUT THE AUTHOR

Audley J. Young was born and raised in the vibrant culture of Jamaica, where the rich traditions of storytelling first sparked a love for weaving tales. In 2005, Audley J. Young moved to the Netherlands, where the blend of cultures and experiences further fueled his imagination.

An everyday tech specialist by profession, Audley discovered a passion for writing in 2020. Balancing the worlds of technology and creativity, Audley enjoys crafting stories that bring joy, laughter, and valuable lessons to young readers.

Audley's believes in the power of stories to teach important values in a fun and engaging way. When not immersed in the tech world or working on the next story, Audley enjoys exploring the diverse landscapes of the Netherlands and reminiscing about the colorful beauty of his homeland Jamaica.